HOW TO
WORK FROM
HOME BETTER

AARRON DANN

DEDICATION

For Reno, The Dollies
and Teddy Boy

CONTENTS

Acknowledgements · i

Introduction · 1

1 Create a positive working environment · 3

2 Manage your time effectively · 25

3 Establish good communication skills · 45

4 Improve your work-life balance · 69

5 Implement sustainable and lasting changes · 83

Summary · 97

ACKNOWLEDGEMENTS

Thank you to the friends and colleagues that provided me with the opportunity to work from home from the other side of the world, and for the trust that they showed in me to make it a success.

INTRODUCTION

**'In the long history of humankind those who
learned to collaborate and improvise most
effectively have prevailed'**
Charles Darwin

I spent a decade working remotely from my home in
Australia for my full-time employer on the other side of
the world in London. During this time I learnt countless
new skills and disciplines that are required for
successfully working from home in a global and virtual
context, plus I was able to enjoy a very positive work-
life balance.

But this book is not about me. It is about you; and an
important point to make is that the ideas that we will
introduce to you should be used as 'blue-prints' with
which to overlay on to your own life and your own
individual set of circumstances.

In this book we will look at some best-practice ways of
working and communicating in the working from home
environment. We will also be looking at how to make
the most of the opportunity to work from home and
how to use it to achieve a greater work-life balance.

Lastly, we'll look at the process of establishing new habits and behaviours that will enable you to achieve the maximum success in this new way of working and living.

There are many different reasons that people may be working from home. Perhaps you are part of a flexible working arrangement and working from home one day a week, or maybe you are part of a full-time home based deployment, or possibly you are working independently as a home based business owner or as a sales consultant. Whatever your situation you will find this book to be of great value in assisting you to work from home more effectively and, as a result, enabling you to enjoy improved professional and personal success.

1. CREATE A POSITIVE WORKING ENVIRONMENT

'No matter where you go; there you are'
Confucius

In order to create success, you need to first create the right conditions for success, so it is important that you pay attention to creating the best environment for you to work in.

Regardless of whether you are working from home all of the time or just some of the time, I would suggest that you set up your home-office so that it is suitable for you to work full-time from that location, this way you are creating a working environment on the best possible footing. If you create a work-space with a mind-set of only using it sometimes then you will be compromising right from the outset. The idea of 'working from home' already exists in our minds in a certain way, and the space that we have established in our homes will reflect our attitudes towards it; those attitudes will need redefining if you are to optimise your performance and improve your effectiveness in working remotely.

The creation of permanent and productive work-space in your home needs to represent the physical manifestation of a shift in attitude towards working from home. It is no longer something you may do one day a week in an unstructured and random way, it isn't something you'll do for an hour or so when you have some work to catch up on for a big meeting. This is now somewhere in your home where, regardless of how much time you will be spending there, you will need to be entirely focused and 'at work.'

When considering the task of creating a new workplace it is important to look at prioritisation and consider what comes first in order that we create an environment that will produce our best results.

'Maslow's hierarchy of needs' is a standardised way of looking at how human needs are prioritised in their most basic form. It was developed by Abraham Maslow in 1943 and takes the shape of a pyramid that shows man's most basic needs at the bottom. It shows that our first priority is our physiological needs (air, water, food for our survival and a roof over our heads for protection) and then, once these have been taken care of, we then require our safety needs to be assured (safety in our home, job security and financial stability).

It is not until these first two sets of basic requirements are fulfilled that we even consider moving on to the other things that are essential to the success of our working from home. Things such as belongingness, self-esteem and creativity will all be required in working from home. These take the form of; positive communication ability, individual self-confidence, personal resilience skills, creative problem solving and independent self-management.

Maslow's theory is still used often today because it reminds us of the importance of creating environments that take care of our most basic needs first, as without doing so, we will not be creating an environment that has the right conditions for us to interact and perform effectively. There are prerequisite levels of requirements in our immediate surroundings that, if not met, will inhibit our ability to mentally and physically relax enough to move on to the next levels.

Your working environment is such a crucial part of making this evolution a success. The environment that you create for your work will be a critical first part in establishing the boundaries between 'work and 'home.' So let's look at the requirements for this space.

Consider comfort

Carl Jung spoke about 'the collective unconscious' which refers to structures of the unconscious mind that are shared among beings of the same species. These common strings of thought are all shared collectively by humankind in our unconscious thoughts and combine to produce a single source of shared thoughts and ideas. Today we have Google. Doing a Google image search is always a good way to see how we perceive things in our collective 'image-bank'. If you did a Google image search for 'working from home' the results would show pictures of people with their laptops who are lying on the floor, on the sofa, in bed, in the garden, on the beach, perhaps with a happy baby on their lap and countless other completely unpractical positions and locations in which to spend eight hours a day.

We look at these images and we understand that they are just models who are in those poses to inspire a positive idea of working from home that is harmonious with a great lifestyle. What they don't show is how that beautiful model looks after eight hours of lying on the cold floor, on her belly, working on her laptop. They don't show exactly how much work that handsome dad got done while he was balancing the baby on his lap while working on his laptop. Sure we're intelligent enough to not take these images as 'fact' but they do demonstrate a collective idea that working from home is transient, that it is over pretty quickly and it is something that we simply juggle with our home life.

The time duration is one aspect that we need to redefine in working from home effectively. You will be doing this for a significant amount of time, some for up to forty hours per week and more. So one of your basic requirements is to make sure that you are physically comfortable. You will need a chair and a desk that are suitable for your needs. This may sound obvious but so often people adapt by repurposing a table to use as their desk and sit on anything that they can find around the house.

Remember, this is not 'home' this is 'work'. If you went in to the office and they gave you an old kitchen table and a stool to sit on for eight hours a day, then I'm sure you'd be a little unhappy about it. You'd be even less happy when they dumped the washing basket and the kid's toys on your desk too. Yet when we set up an office at home, we make the same mistakes with our furniture as we do with our attitude; we adapt our 'home' to fit in the 'work'. This room and this furniture is not 'home' it is 'work.'

Make sure it is suitable for your specific work

Home-offices are becoming an increasingly common feature in many of our homes. Many modern homes have home-offices included as a part of their design layout and many of us have adapted a spare room to use as a home-office. However, many of these spaces have been created on the basis of them being somewhere to do a little work when required but perhaps not used on a full-time basis.

Quite often they are perfect for the odd day working from home every now and again or to prepare for a big meeting but perhaps not always somewhere to be able to really focus and feel like you are 'at work.' Often they are multi-purpose rooms and are somewhere to file the 'business' side of home life (tax returns, bank statements etc), somewhere for the kids to do their homework and for mum and dad to catch up on work stuff.

When you are selecting a location in your home in which to create your full-time workspace you need to identify your needs and create your new workspace in the location that is best suited to take care of those needs. This may or may not be the existing home-office. If it has been somewhere that has been suitable for ad-hoc home working or multi-purpose family use then these are very different requirements and it may not match your new requirements of somewhere to really focus and to work most effectively.

If it's choice was based on it simply being the 'spare room' then, again, this may not mean that it is necessarily a suitable location. Likewise if the choice of location for the home-office was made because that was on the house build-plan then it may not be right either.

So, what are the new requirements? Make a list. In compiling this list it may be worth referring back to your current office work environment or previous full-time workplace. What was good, what was bad? Whatever your particular profession it's likely that the need to concentrate will be required, so therefore your working environment will need to be quiet. If the current home-office is next to your play room, or situated close to your neighbours noisy air-conditioning unit, then this may not be the best place to concentrate fully on your work commitments.

Depending on the sort of fixtures you'd like to include in your work-space, it is unlikely that it will need to be the largest room in the house. Generally home-offices can be quite small as they will often only need to accommodate a single desk. However, do you want to feel like you are shut in a cupboard in your home working life?

What about the view? It's nice to have a good view to look out at but will it distract you from your work? Sunlight? It's important to select a room that is going to provide you with enough sunlight (and not starve yourself of those important endorphins that natural light produces in us) but often the glare of direct sunlight can result in headaches for computer based workers. Also, will direct sunlight affect the legibility of your computer screen?

Put together your list of requirements, that may include some of the ones that we have mentioned. Select the room that is best suited to meet those requirements and then give it a try. It's possible that there will be no perfect place and, if there is, you may not get it right first time. Therefore after trying one particular location you may need to add some additional requirements to your list that you've become aware of. Then you can see if they can be met elsewhere, or simply adapt as best you can. For example if the room is just too noisy because it is the closest room to the road outside and it's just a lot busier than you thought (because you've perhaps only experienced it at weekends before), then you may need to try another room. Or it could be that most things are fine but at a certain time of day the sun comes through the window and you can't see your screen very well. So it may be that you adapt by simply closing the curtains for that period of time each day.

Connection to your workplace

In this digital age it is great that we can successfully work remotely from our office, however this situation does put a greater dependency on the reliability and efficiency of the technology that we rely on to make it work. If your link with your office is digital (and there is a pretty strong chance that it will be) then I would definitely recommend that your make sure your home location has robust and reliable Internet connections. I don't just mean simply 'can you get online'. Internet speeds vary around the world and, depending on the kind of work you do this may affect your day-to-day activity. I would recommend that you do adequate due diligence on this key fundamental or it could potentially disrupt your working life and sabotage your efforts in creating an effective work from home situation.

Make it as separate from your home environment as possible

Ironically, the ideal place for a home-office will often be outside of the home. If you are fortunate enough to have an external building or room that can be converted for use then that would be perfect (somewhere like a no-longer-used den or summer-house, or a work-shop adjoining your garage). The reason being, that it makes it so much easier to separate the two entities of your life if you have to physically go outside of the home to get to work. The mental attitude and time management is made much easier by the physical and geographical segmentation.

Regardless of where your home-office is (whether it's inside the home or outside), I would encourage an attitude of your office being considered as *separate* from your home. Many of the attitudes and behaviours that are required in successfully working from home depend on your ability to separate the two different parts of your life. This is made easier if you discipline yourself to act in a way that supports this. Developing the mind-set that 'work is work and home is home' gives you the best possible chance to get the most out of these areas and avoids the very real danger of compromising on both. This theme of successful segmentation and self-discipline is a consistent one that we will come back to again, and being able to instill this mind-set early on gives you a good foundation with which to establish new habits in your attitude and in your behaviour.

View it as an opportunity
Did you ever look enviously at your boss's plush office with their expensive desk, their stylish pictures on the wall and tasteful furniture around the room? Well you no longer need to wait to be given an office like that; you can just create it yourself.

Did you ever watch a movie or TV show that featured a great looking office and compared it to your own workspace in the reality of your working life? The silver screen rarely represents anything by chance. If a character in a story is successful then he or she will inhabit a beautiful office space that represents their power, their success and their wealth. If a character is not so successful then it is likely that he or she will inhabit a small cubicle in an open-plan office. This will represent their humble position in the organisation and their modest level of success in life. This is simple image-association that we all understand and yet it works with all of us. We will watch these characters and understand the symbolism embedded in the environment that they inhabit, and yet when it comes to reality, there is not always such a clear set of rules.

In real life many working environments are open-plan and it is not uncommon for all employees to populate a small cubicle, regardless of their position. It is often the case that the boss will be sitting next to his or her team, with no obvious distinction between their positions in the organisation. Those same wonderful offices that we see in the movies often have beautiful cityscape views from their windows. In reality many working environments have a very different view. Sure, some may have a cityscape view but many will look out to a busy road, a soulless industrial estate and many do not have a view at all. Some people's working environments have no windows and no natural light coming in. There are as many different working environments as there are people in the workplace, and each one will be different.

As our working environments are often shared with others, we often have to compromise our own needs in consideration for others. Some people may sit right next to a window and, at certain times of day be faced with the direct glare of sunlight, but are not able to adjust the blinds because it will detrimentally affect others. Some people sit directly under a heater or air conditioning unit and although they get the full force of it, they have to consider that the heat or warmth is for everybody and so they will need to perhaps deal with it by wearing a coat all day. In the case of open-plan offices it sometimes happens that people are located next to one another and the nature of their different working remits do not work well together. For example, a team of programmers may be located together in the office but the person at the outer area of that group may be located next to the sales team. The programmer needs quiet in order that they can concentrate on their work. The sales team needs to talk to clients on the phone all day in order to sell the product that the programmers are busy creating. Sure there are always headphones and work-arounds but these are examples of situations that commonly occur through having to share our working environment and how this can result in our own needs being compromised.

You now have the opportunity to create it the way you want it. It is entirely yours and it can potentially be the office that you've always wanted or perhaps similar to a working environment that you've seen portrayed on the TV and that you will enjoy spending time in and will help to make you feel successful. Getting a workspace right-for-purpose is a challenge: Being able to create a whole new environment that reflects your working life and your attitude and behaviours towards it; that's an opportunity, and your own attitude towards your workspace will be a direct reflection of your (and everybody else's) attitude towards your work. If it is a lowly regarded, messy area of the house (that may be used for other things as well) then that is how your work will be viewed within your household. You cannot expect others to respect the professional aspect of your life and your identity, if you do not respect it yourself.

The way you set up your workspace is the foundation for establishing how your work will be viewed.

Make it a positive environment
Spending so much time working alone can sometimes be daunting and feelings can often become magnified. Consider how sometimes you're worrying about something and it keeps you awake at night. It can be the same in a lonely home-office if you let it. Time spent alone often increases the intensity of the thoughts that dominate our day, so try and make these thoughts predominantly positive. Magnifying these in your head can be great, but magnifying insecurities and doubts can be corrosive, and have the potential to ultimately destroy your attitude and performance at work.

The things that determine your experience most dominantly will be the thoughts and feelings that accompany you throughout your working day. If you have a positive association with the idea of working from home then that is a good foundation to build a positive and proactive attitude with which to embrace the challenge and seek success. If, however, you have a negative association with the concept then this is likely to hold you back and make success harder to achieve. Whatever your own attitudes, they will play a significant part in producing your outcomes - good or bad.

We all deal with change in different ways. Some of us may relish the opportunity to enjoy a more flexible arrangement in our working lives, while others may struggle with the idea and feel isolated from the familiar conventions of their working day.

Another factor that may determine how we feel about working from home is our age and often the older we get, the harder it becomes for us to learn new things. Those fresh young brain-cells that we took so much for granted at school are now not so young and fresh anymore. For many of us, life's changes are not so easy to embrace as we get older.

Douglas Adams, the writer of 'The Hitchhikers Guide to the Galaxy' said the following three rules govern how people react to change and technology:

1. Anything that is in the world when you're born is normal and ordinary and is just a natural part of the way the world works.

2. Anything that is invented between when you're 15 and 35 years old is new and exciting and revolutionary, and you can probably get a career in it.

3. Anything invented after you're 35 is against the natural order of things.

Surrounding yourself with positive things in your working environment encourages positive feelings.
However, there is only so much that happy photographs and inspirational posters can do to create a positive environment for you to work in. Creating a positive working environment is as much about the feelings and attitudes that you bring in to your home-office space as the fixtures and fittings that you choose to fill it with.

Introverts and extroverts
Consider if you are an 'introvert' or an 'extrovert'. We

tend to have stereotypical images of introverts and extroverts and tend think to that these are conscious ways of behaving. But whether we are introvert or extrovert is actually stamped in to our DNA, and will be a constant throughout our lives.

Research shows that introverts tend to be much better suited to working from home than extroverts. Personally I do not like the idea that I am an introvert as it conjures images of someone who is shy and awkward but, looking at the definition, I probably do match that profile. The definition of an introvert, in this context, is somebody who is focused, creative and actually works best making independent decisions without the need for peer approval.

Extroverts on the other hand need to be around other people and thrive on the interaction that it brings. They do not deal well with making decisions independently of others as they need the collaboration and the recognition that comes with it. It's interesting that, statistically, there are many extroverts who become entrepreneurs and actually struggle with the isolation and so return to an office based environment. They are attracted to the image of it (being the boss of a large company with lots of employees) but the environment that is required to bring that situation about is not something that they enjoy (working alone and making independent decisions). What type are you?

Are you an optimistic or a pessimistic person?
Our preconceptions lead us to believe that optimists are better at dealing with challenges because they 'don't worry' about the outcome as much as pessimists do.

However, research actually shows that the difference between an optimistic attitude and a pessimistic attitude is not that simple. For example; it's been discovered that optimists generally live longer than pessimists, but not for the simplistic reason of worrying less about dying. The research demonstrates that the reason is that the optimists *believe* that they will live longer and so that belief creates the actions that will bring that reality about (they actively take vitamins, eat healthier, they do more exercise and so on.) The scientist Ajit Varki of the University of California believes that 'optimism is denying reality.' So, if our level of optimism is simply based on our perception of reality then whose reality is the most accurate? Their research discovered that:

People with 'severe depression' - Expect things to be worse than they end up being.

People with 'mild depression' – Have a pretty accurate expectation and prediction of the future.

People who are 'optimists' - Expect the future to be better than it ends up being.

If you are looking for your working from home to have a successful outcome then obviously you will need to develop a positively orientated attitude towards it. With your behaviour being so influenced by your attitude and mind-set, you will struggle to make anything a success if your actions are positive but your underlying belief system doesn't match it. If you apply the attitude of an optimist and expect positive outcomes, then your response to any setback is healthier. If you apply the attitude of a pessimist then your response to negative outcomes is 'great, just as I expected.'

We have to work with how we are by nature and just because you may have a tendency towards pessimism it doesn't necessarily mean that you can never make a success of this, but rather that you may need to adapt your behaviour to help produce positive outcomes. We are what we are, and it is no good claiming to be an optimist just because you think that is the right answer. It is better to be honest with yourself and understand where you may encounter increased difficulties or stress as, that way, you can then recognize where you may need to adapt.

The important thing to learn from this is that an optimistic attitude will not bring about less challenges or problems, in itself. However, brain-scans show that when optimists make mistakes activity sparks up in the part of the brain that deals with self-reflection and recollection, whereas brain-scans show no increased brain activity in pessimists after making mistakes.

The reality of an optimist will be no better or worse in the short-term than that of a pessimist. However, their reality does ultimately improve because their response to setbacks is to ask why and so they fix the problem and improve their reality in the longer term. So, the research here demonstrates that optimists have greater self-confidence as a result of the ability to deploy more resilience. Pessimistic behaviour patterns tend to passively accept bad news and don't try to change it. This is demonstrated in the following research findings from Duke University:

Optimists and pessimists share the same probability in getting divorced.
However, optimists are more likely to get remarried

As is often the case, these research findings serve to clarify something that we instinctively understand already, and they were articulated well by Winston Churchill, who said; 'A pessimist sees the difficulty in every opportunity; an optimist sees the opportunity in every difficulty.'

Are you self-confident and resilient?

Working alone not only requires a certain amount of independence in our attitudes and actions, but it also requires some degree of confidence and belief in our own abilities. This is required in order that we can embrace these new challenges and seek to bring about positive outcomes. What is your own self-confidence level like? It may be that you have great confidence in your ability to perform the tasks of your job in any environment - great. Or it may be that you are confident in what you do, but are not so sure how you will be able to adapt, and if you'll enjoy the same level of confidence in a working from home environment.

Given what we have just learnt about the difference between optimists and pessimists it shows us that optimists demonstrate more resilience. Whether our natural orientation is of a pessimistic or optimistic nature, if we know that deploying some resilience serves us better in a working from home environment then we should be looking to adapt our behaviour appropriately. If it is indeed true, or we at least subscribe to the belief, that; 'Fear of failure is the greatest barrier to success' then we need to try and lessen our fear of the possibility of failure, and see this as a part of the overall development process that we will need to go through in order to achieve success.

So if we are accepting the fact that it is probable that we will encounter some degree of failure then we will need to deploy some resilience in putting these setbacks in perspective; learn from them, and then move forward with a greater understanding. How is your resilience? How do you feel about being faced with new challenges that may result in one or two failures or mistakes? Can you learn from these and understand that they may be a necessary part of finding your way towards positive results?

Moving forward
The advice I've shared with you is based on best practice learnt through experience, with a little common sense thrown in there. The aim is to try and help you get it right first time and help your transition to an effective home working environment. However in reality, everybody's situation is different and there may not be a perfect scenario to begin with. In which case, the important thing is that you adapt positively and work towards an optimum situation with your specific requirements in mind.

For example, when I first began working from home full-time I had a far from perfect working environment. It was a small and very old house that we were renovating. In the summer months it was extremely hot, as we had no air-conditioning, and the exposed beams meant that we had no roof and ceiling insulation. Also, our youngest child was a pre-school toddler. The result was that my working environment meant using a room that we combined as a living room, bedroom and home-office. The house was infested with wildlife that had been disrupted by our renovations and on one occasion I had a deadly spider crawl up my leg while I was busy working. On another occasion, the heat was such that a thick candle melted before my eyes through the course of a particularly hot working day.

The situation could not be improved upon in the short-term and so I had to adapt and work towards an improved longer-term solution with my new understanding of the importance of needing a workspace that was conducive to full-time home based working. I had fans on myself and on my laptop for eight hours a day. I wore a pilot headset to block-out the noise of 'Bob the Builder' on the TV, and I kept a weathered eye out for various forms of wildlife. When that house was renovated we sold it and looked for a new home with a clear specification of a home-office that was high on the priority list. We then bought our next home that had a room that was perfect as a home-office, and I worked there happily for many years.

Allow time to adapt

Although we have covered many things in creating a positive working environment we cannot account for every possible scenario that may occur, and there will be a unique set of circumstances for each different person. It is possible that there will be things that are causing you problems that no amount of planning or preparation could avoid. Perhaps the neighbour's toddler keeps crying or there is a dog down the road that just won't stop barking. These are things that cannot be avoided and the reality is that you are now working in an alien environment to what you have been conditioned to.

Wherever home is for you, it is likely that it will be very different to the working environment that you are familiar with. The suburbs are not designed for homeworkers and, as annoying as it may be, toddlers will cry and dogs will bark. They are not the ones out of place, you are; and so you are the one that is going to have to adapt. You are the square peg fitting in to a round hole and as much preparation as you have done (making your home-office as conducive to work as possible etc) you have to accept that you are working in an environment that has not been created exclusively for work. You are sharing it with others that are using it for life.

Turning your world upside down
If this all sounds a bit gloomy then don't worry, you will adapt - it will just take some time for the unfamiliar to become familiar. If it feels like your world has been turned upside down then consider this experiment that NASA carried out with their astronauts:

In order to test the impact of spatial disorientation NASA fitted a group of astronauts with convex goggles that flipped everything by 180 degrees, so literally turning their world upside down. These test subjects wore these glasses 24 hours a day and their physiological and psychological reactions were observed. The results showed that the stress and anxiety levels started out extremely high but then, over time, the anxiety lessened but did not disappear altogether. The astronauts were dealing with this new environment but they were certainly not enjoying it.

Then after 26 days something amazing happened. One particular astronaut reported that his world had turned right side up again, and over the following days the other subjects reported the same results. What the experiment had shown was that over a 26 - 30 day period the brains of the astronauts had created enough new neural connections to rewire their brains and fully recalibrate their perception in response to this new 'reality'. Their brain had reprogrammed everything so that their upside down world had been turned the right way around.

If you stay positive and apply yourself consistently towards working from home effectively then the results will come.

2. MANAGE YOUR TIME EFFECTIVELY

'Focusing is about saying no'
Steve Jobs

The importance of mastering the art of time management is more crucial than ever in this new mode of working from home, where the lines between work and life have become blurred.

'Parkinson's Law' states that any task expands or contracts to fill the time made available for it. This is a very useful thing to be aware of when we are forced to produce something within a short time-frame. If we know that we only have a certain amount of time available to us then we will do whatever it takes to make it happen within that time-frame – and we generally get it done. However, the inverse effect of the law is something to be aware of too; in that whatever time you allow for a task is how long it will take. If a child has an hour of homework to do at the weekend and they get it done before 9am on Saturday then the weekend is theirs to do with as they wish. If however they just decide that they'll get it done 'at some point' over the weekend then they are making the whole weekend *available* for their homework. As a result their entire weekend will be spent 'working' because that is the time frame that they specified for the task.

This is a very relevant situation for those of us who are working from home, and never more so than in today's world where we are connected by technology and *available* for work 24/7. If the time available for work is not established clearly then it will simply expand to fill all of our time, and 'work' will inevitably flow over in to 'life.'

So how do you manage this situation? Do you make a fuss about how unfair it is that you're available for work 24/7? Do you put up with it but have a festering resentment that your working life has eroded your home life? No, you accept this situation as a reality (that has simply been brought about by the same technology that enables you the opportunity to work from anywhere in the world) and you define a structure for your working day and your working life.

Defining time

Time has no intrinsic value, in itself. It is like money; the pieces of currency themselves have no actual value - they are simply a means of exchange. It is only by using those coins and notes that money takes on any meaning. It is exactly the same with time (and they even both share the same phraseology); by *spending* money, we give it meaning and so too by *spending* time we give it meaning and value.

If we simply let our money fall through a hole in our pockets then we will never know we had it and it will never make any significant impact in our lives. We will be doing the same with our time if we just let it slip away without our noticing – never knowing we had it, and so it never making any significant impact in our lives. Sadly most of us are guilty of this to some extent and although we will all nod our heads and agree with such sentiments as 'time is the most priceless commodity', we generally take it for granted and assume it will last forever.

It is only when we are faced with the finite aspect of time; at moments such as illness, aging and even death, do we realise that it will not last forever. 'Live each day as if it's your last' we may have on a pin-board, but how often do any of us actually live each day like that?

Understanding your accountability

Do you actually know what the expectations are from you in the time that you spend working from home? If not, then a very important thing that I would recommend is that you take some time to define your 'performance metrics.' By really looking to identify the ways which your performance will be judged, you'll be giving yourself and your boss a measurable gauge with which to determine your output levels. This should enable you to have a better understanding of what is expected of you and some objective accountability. It'll also provide you with some targets to beat - with your work time now being more focused and productive.

Defining performance metrics is easier for some than others and certain work is just not easy to identify as a set of individual tasks. One of the things that remote working radically challenges is how our efficiency is managed and recorded and in particular with the often used gauge of measuring 'output by input.' With a remote worker not being there in the office, it is not easy for their manager to see that they are actually working. Our conventional way of measuring an employee's efficiency is to see how many hours they are sitting at their desk although, as we know, this is not an accurate indicator of how much work is actually getting done. It's not always easy for businesses to measure output and so, instead, input is often focused on as the performance metric. For example, if somebody does the same amount of work in four days as it takes another to do in six days, then it will be the latter that is best received as he worked all week, and even put in a day at the weekend. This is a way of thinking that is difficult to shift in the workplace.

It's not surprising that input is often judged more than output as, without accurate metrics for measurement, much of this judgment happens on a subconscious level. Let's look at a scenario of three workers who all produce identical output, but have different levels of input. If I am a manager and I see employee one in the office every day, then I will think of them as 'dependable'. If I see employee two there in the office every day and some evenings as well, then I think of them as 'committed'. If I do not see employee three there all of the time (as they spend some time working from home) then subconsciously I may not feel that they are as committed or dependable as the rest of my team, although their productivity is exactly the same. While it is useful to recognise that this situation may exist, it is important to understand that, as it happens on a subconscious level, it is not intentional and so try not to take it personally. What you need to do is to try and establish a gauge that quantifies your work output with an objective 'level playing field' mechanism that avoids these subconscious input-based judgments.

As well as understanding our own accountability and recognising what we are personally responsible for, it is also important to understand the 'chain of accountability' that we are part of. As children, we have a simplistic view that there are employees and 'the boss.' The reality is, in most organisations, everybody has a boss and you have to go a long way up the chain of command before you get to the 'big boss,' and even he or she potentially has bosses in the form of shareholders. We are all accountable to somebody else and, when you work from home, your boss will need to have a good handle on your efficiency levels in order to report to their boss (who in turn reports to theirs and so it goes on). Personally I found that, having been a manager myself, it was much easier for me to understand what my manager would want to see from me in terms of efficiency and productivity. I understood that he wasn't asking because he was judging me or he wanted to give me a hard time but simply because my accountability to him was directly related to his accountability to his boss, and so on.

Discipline and focus

Discipline is obviously something that some of us are better at than others. We all have our temptations and these will be different for everybody. There will be as many different things that tempt people as there are the things that inspire people. It is important to recognise what you personally need to discipline yourself against. What are your temptations? What will be whispering in your ear when you're trying to work? Will you be tempted, without a boss around to stop you?

One of the reasons that we can potentially work more effectively from a home-office is that we have the opportunity to be able to focus our thoughts and our attentions. For many of us our office based working day is filled with disruptions and distractions and it is very common for people to be introduced to the opportunity of working from home (on a flexible, part-time basis) and discover that they get so much more work done. Without the interruptions, that we have come to accept as part of our working day, we find the opportunity to really focus enables us to get work done quicker and more fluidly.

Whether at work or at home, there will always be something to attract your attention but, as Steve Jobs said, 'Focusing is about saying no.'

The culture of 'busyness'
The nature of working from home will require you to spend more time alone and, therefore you will need to enjoy your own company. This is something that many of us are becoming increasingly uncomfortable with and the digital technology that enables us to work from home is the same technology that constantly gives us the excuse to not spend any time with ourselves. For some of us, the relationship with ourselves has become like an awkward Uncle that you don't want to be left alone with because you don't know what to say to him. The digital tools that we have at our disposal enable us to successfully avoid spending anytime with ourselves.

We have embraced these tools of connectivity, noise and activity to the extent that we are finding ourselves living our lives more and more *virtually* and less and less *actually*.

This is not only causing problems at a social level, it also means that we are not putting our brains in to a valuable 'off mode' and are therefore missing out on some of our brain's less tangible capacities. Thinking creatively and fostering new ideas, taking time to consider events and learn from experiences, understanding your own feelings and priorities, and the ability to appreciate the moment: These are all important ways of engaging our brains for our own well-being and personal development, and they are things that we do when our brain is disengaged from its duties in our work capacity. Our brains need an appropriate amount of down-time and this is something you need to consider in your time management.

In today's world we are surrounded with gadgets designed to give us more time. Ironically, we find ourselves busier than ever, and much of this is because of the habits that we have developed in our use of these devices. Many of us have forgotten how to let our brains go to 'idle' mode. This idle mode is when our subconscious kicks in and gives our conscious brains a rest. This is the same subconscious brain that deals with all of our creativity, our memory and plays an important part in forming the very ideas that make up who we are.

When we are no longer working, we all too often reach for the mobile device to find some distraction for our brains. It is rare that we allow ourselves time for our minds to just wander; but these are the times when we come up with our best ideas, consider our responses to events unemotionally and feel at our most relaxed. These habits of behaviour may have been formed for different reasons; for some of us it is the need to feel 'busy and important', the habits of others may have been developed to feel 'needed' and then there is the curse of 'FOMO' (the fear of missing out). The different types of distractions will vary also. It may be that you habitually check the news on the Internet, it may be that you're checking your social media sites for gossip or it may simply be that you feel the need to kill off any silence with music. However these patterns of behaviour have been formed, they all result in the same thing, and that is the avoidance of engaging our subconscious mind.

Many people believe that we have developed a culture of 'busyness' and in his book 'Autopilot – the art and science of doing nothing' Andrew Smart says; 'In order to function normally our brains also need to be idle.' He also goes on to say; 'In the short-term busyness destroys creativity, self-knowledge, emotional well-being, your ability to be social – and it can damage your cardiovascular system.' Another subscriber to the belief that the culture of busyness is detrimental to our well-being is the writer Richard Newton who believes that we have developed an abject fear of being bored. In his book entitled 'The little book of thinking big' he says; 'Noticing, contemplation, inspiration, the next big thing often arises out of boredom; an unsung champion of thinking big. Smartphones have sucked the juice out of boredom. What used to be rich and fertile compost for idle noticing, and contemplation is now desiccated.'

The importance of compartmentalisation

Where previously our work lives and home lives were separated by time and location, today they are becoming increasingly interwoven. We used to start and finish our work at certain times and, when the working day was done, we would not think about it again until it resumed again. Now we find the world's workforce logged on to their work server on the train journey in to work, being emailed at all hours via their smart phones and when work isn't interrupting their home lives they feel compelled to 'just check their emails to make sure everything is ok.'

This is becoming an increasingly common scenario for many of us and is not only taking chunks out of our time at home; we are even doing it on our holidays. Our work-life balance is becoming increasingly skewed; our stress levels are at an all-time high and our health and fitness is suffering as a consequence. This situation has come about while we were located in a workplace. How on earth can the situation improve when we find ourselves working from home and the last barrier between work life and home life has been removed?

This situation does not apply to everyone and, for some, it may seem I perhaps paint a pretty bleak picture. However, I describe this situation for a reason; and that is, when you work from home, you have an opportunity to reset the dial and to avoid this situation either being created or getting worse for you. In the ten years that I spent working from home as a full-time employee, I was always very rigid in my organisation and compartmentalisation between work and life. I believe this is one of the real keys in making working from home a success. Earlier on we were introduced to 'Parkinson's Law' which, you may remember, tells us that any task expands or contracts to fill the time made available for it. Compartmentalisation is an excellent mechanism for avoiding the scenario where we are always *available* for work and so as a result our work expands to fill our entire lives.

Something that I came to recognise early on in my time working from home was that, without the journey home, there was no clear differentiation between work time and home time. I therefore created activities that would denote that work had ended and home time had begun. I would go to the park or the beach with my kids, walk my dog, go for a run or perhaps take a swim. I would generally change the activity but I did find that it needed to be a physical activity and ideally one in a different location to home. The physical activities such as running or swimming would enable me to 'flush through' my working day by allowing me to give some reflection to the day and offload any physical stress. The other activities with my family would enable me to place my full attention elsewhere and leave work behind for the day. Some people may be different but, for me, after being conditioned by countless years of commuting home, I found that my body and mind needed some activity to be placed in between work time and home time that would serve as a transition from one mind-set to the other, and hopefully be fun too.

These are activities that suited my personality and I enjoyed doing, but for you there may be different activities that you enjoy and benefit from in a similar way. The point here is not the nature of the activity, but rather the importance of putting something in place that helps to define the parameters of your working day and helps to establish new positive patterns of behaviour. Another thing that I have always done is to change clothes. When I finished work I would always change clothes to reinforce the fact that work was now finished and life had begun. Again, this is a small thing but it really makes it easier to create these new behaviour patterns if we are making physical changes that our minds and bodies can easily understand.

Something else that I did when I had finished work was to close the laptop and lock my office door. This way work was finished and, at weekends, I would not check work emails or messages. These physical actions made it easier for me to develop the necessary discipline. These ways became habits and I did it consistently for all of the years that I worked from home. I know that everybody's situation is different and I can almost hear the outraged cries of 'my boss would never let me be uncontactable'. However, while there is no 'one-size-fits-all' solution, I would encourage an awareness of the principles of Parkinson's Law and would also say that we are each ultimately responsible for our own work-life balance. The boundaries that we establish at the start will form the ongoing expectations of us. If you do not decide on your work-life balance then nobody else will do it for you. No matter how disciplined any of us are, the importance of putting firm rules and activities in place to encourage compartmentalisation cannot be understated.

The danger of compromise

Do not compromise: Give your full attention to work and then your full attention to home.

Most of us have two very different 'hats' that we wear for life at work and life outside of work. What I mean is that we have two very different versions of us in the two different environments. These will include different demeanour, attitude, response mechanism to events, ways of managing various situations, and so on. Our home life is often a place of emotion and feelings. We may feel that we can happily relax, surrounded by our loved ones. It is predominantly about feelings as opposed to thoughts – it is somewhere where we feel we can switch off and enjoy our 'down-time.' Our workplace on the other hand is dominated by objectivity and is more thought and action orientated. We know our duties and we assess situations in a more objective manner before developing our responses and applying our actions accordingly.

It is important to retain that objective attitude in your workplace, now that it is embedded in your home environment. Identify the hat that you have worn in the workplace, and that has suited that environment. Make sure that you bring that 'work hat' with you to your home working environment and that you continue wearing it when you are working. Remember, when you are working you are not at home, you are at work. When you have finished work then you can 'go home' and change hats.

When you are at work you need to be 100% focused on your work, and when you are at home you need to be 100% focused on your life. Why compromise your attention by giving 80% of your focus to your work while you listen to your child tell you about their school day with the remaining 20%? Give 100% focus to your work and then, when the working day is finished, give 100% focus to your child and listen properly to them talk about their day at school. It is better to do one thing well than lots of things badly. Your employer will not thank you for trying to juggle everything and be a super hero and nor will your family.

Your employer pays you to be working for them during the hours of your contract, and in that time they will expect 100% of your time and commitment to be dedicated to the remit that you have within the organisation. Your family may be somewhat different, depending on the individual circumstances of your household. For example young kids will probably not understand the concept of you being at home but 'unavailable' to be their parent. This is where those rules and boundaries are so important and that everybody in your household needs to know that when you are at work you are at work, and when you are at home you are at home. This can only be upheld by your being consistent with it. If you keep moving the goalposts then how will anybody know when they can talk to you and when they cannot?

This does not have to be a heavy-handed rule where your kids feel may that you are punishing them or that you don't want to see them. They just need to understand that you are busy at work, just as you would be if you were in a different location. The best way to deal with this is to make sure that you are giving them your undivided attention when you are home; no checking emails, no popping back in to the home-office to update a document with something that has just popped in to your head. This doesn't just apply to young kids, this will apply to anyone that you share your home life with. They will accept your needing to commit yourself to work if they feel that you are wholly committed to them when you are not at work. If your family feels that you working from home compromises their time and relationship with you then it is likely that resentment will develop and that working from home will be seen as the thing that is responsible. This is not true; it will be your inability in manage your time and your commitments that are responsible.

Compromising your time and your commitments is a common contemporary problem and so many things are blamed for it; demanding bosses, demanding spouses, demanding kids and so on. As a result we often feel that we have so little time available and so we try and juggle everybody to make them all happy. Unfortunately what tends to happen is that we succeed in making nobody happy; because our efforts to take care of everybody's needs at once result in us not meeting anybody's needs at all. We don't do one thing well but instead do lots of things badly.

Compromising your time has the ability to seriously damage the likelihood of successfully working from home, and is something we always need to be aware of. The best way to prevent this is to make sure that we have an attitude of full, uncompromised commitment to your work and then a full, uncompromised commitment to your life outside of work - even if life outside work requires relaxing; commit 100% to relaxing, without just popping in to the office.

Understanding the role of technology and managing your relationship with it

Digital communication and how we use it in our lives is such a huge topic and not one that I want to explore in great lengths, but it something that is very relevant when dealing with the subject of working from home.

How much we choose to engage in the digital world is a personal thing and some people love it and some hate it. In the past it has often been viewed as an intergenerational spat, with younger people not understanding the older generation's dislike for it. However, in 2012 Time Magazine undertook a study on global use of digital devices and amongst their findings it reported that 90% of Brazilians and Indians agreed that being constantly connected is 'generally a good thing', and that 76% of Americans felt that being continuously connected was 'a positive part of their lives'. Figures like this demonstrate that the situation has long since moved on from simply being about the younger generation having such a deep relationship with their electronic devices.

For our purposes, we need to focus on understanding the role of digital technology in enabling us to work from home, and how we manage our engagement of it in order to get the best results.

One of the biggest fears for employers in their work

from home initiatives is the lack of accountability, and this situation puts increasing importance on their employees' ability to be self-managing as a part of their overall capability. The concern is that they will not be doing what they are supposed to be doing, and a survey undertaken by salary.com suggests that these concerns are well founded, with 31% of (office based) employees admitting to wasting an average of 30 minutes a day and another 31% admitting to wasting approximately one hour a day. They are easily able to do this without anybody noticing because the non-work activities are often totally indistinguishable from the work activities. This is when they are in the office – how much time will employees be wasting from their home-office?

The technology that enables us to work from home is the very same technology that has the potential to derail it. The big temptation for home based workers is no longer going to the lounge and watching a movie – they can do this, plus be distracted by countless other things on the same devices that they are using for their work. It is very much 'the enemy within.' In order to make working from home a success it is essential that we *master* our relationship with digital communication or we risk becoming a *slave* to it.

Personally I feel that technology receives a lot of unfair blame for the problems in our lives, as it is generally our *use* of technology and our inability to manage it that is the root cause of so many of these problems. Alex Soojung-Kim Pang, author of 'The Distraction Addiction' believes that 'Connection is inevitable. Distraction is a choice.'

Multitasking

A common problem of our digital world is that it fragments our attention. Our attachment to our various digital devices has led us to believe that multitasking is our 'default setting' and, rather than view this as a negative, it actually makes us feel productive and efficient. Ariana Huffington, President of the Huffington Post Media Group; believes that our need to be connected 24/7 is 'Part of our collective delusion that always being connected is the necessary price for achieving success.'

In reality, multitasking makes us less productive and has been shown to diminish our ability to concentrate on one thing at a time. The constant disruptions that we experience compromise our productivity, as we end up making a small amount of progress over several different tasks, leaving essential work unfinished. According to Professor Clifford Nass, of CHIME (Communication between Humans and Interactive Media) at Stanford University; 'Multitasking reduces our ability to distinguish between important and irrelevant information.' Multitasking has been shown to reduce our capacity to complete tasks effectively because, as Professor Nass points out, 'We invariably end up focusing on the things that we are not doing rather than on the task at hand.'

In another study conducted by neuroscientist Professor Earl Miller, at the Massachusetts Institute of Technology, head scans were performed on volunteers to monitor brain activity while multitasking. The results found that while carrying out multiple tasks their brains were only activated by one thing at a time. The results suggest that when our brains are overloaded with competing tasks, it has to alternate between them, causing its capacity to process information to be severely reduced.

This has been found to especially be the case when we try to perform similar tasks at the same time, such as writing a text while responding to an email and talking on the phone. The reason being that these similar tasks require us to use the same part of the brain, and so it results in that part of the brain functioning much slower.

Our brains are also beginning to recognise multitasking as an adverse way that they are required to perform. Glenn Wilson, a psychiatrist at the University of London discovered that just the thought of multitasking can cause the brain to slow down. He found that just by tackling two similar tasks at the same time, your relative IQ can be reduced by up to 10 points. The knock-on effects of this can result in the type of mental fogginess comparable to missing a whole night's sleep.

Industry recognition
Maintaining a healthy work-life balance is important to our health and well-being, but it is also important for our productivity, effectiveness and our performance and potential for success. We need to do all we can to recognise this and, with increasing amounts of research in this area, organisations are beginning to recognise this too. Volkswagen trialed scheduling shutdowns of their employee's emails thirty minutes after their work day ended. BMW have considered implementing a policy that prevents their staff being contacted after

hours and Goldman Sachs have actively encouraged their employees to take breaks and have weekends off.

According to a 2010 study by the US research company, Basex; corporate America is losing nearly $1 trillion in lost work hours due to employees' information overload and the need to constantly be taking time to open and reply to the continuous stream of work and non-work related correspondence. The research concludes that employees are *present* but not always *productive*.

There is always an off-switch
Effective planning and management of time is something that is crucial to successfully working from home, and the management of our relationship with our technological enabler is something that is at the heart of this on-going challenge. The use of security monitoring programmes is on the increase and there are signs that industry is recognising the need to help us all to manage our engagement with technology, but the responsibility is ultimately down to us as individuals. We need to recognise when to turn it off.

3. ESTABLISH GOOD COMMUNICATION SKILLS

'The more we elaborate our means of communication, the less we communicate'
J. B. Priestley

The organisation and structure of the modern workplace has inherently changed, and so the nature of our communication needs to adapt and evolve to be effective in a virtual context.

Our traditional communications

60 - 80% of all our communication is non-verbal. This is mainly our body language and our gestures but it also includes our adornments; things such as jewellery, dress sense and even beards in the case of men. Research shows that we make the vast majority of our judgments based on the way somebody looks and what they are wearing. The way that they move is also significant and the role of body language in our communication is a complex area where we have developed a range of sensors that perceive and translate body motion and gestures.

Clearly with the majority of our traditional communication being non-verbal, that means that much of the range of characteristics traditionally used (such as body language, appearance, smell, adornments etc) are not used in the developing art of virtual communications. However, as it involves a reduced number of communication components it may potentially be simpler for us to decode and to master the art of communication in a virtual context. So let us now look at how we begin to develop effective communication skills for virtual workplace.

The importance of clarity

An absolute imperative of communicating within the virtual workplace is clarity. Obviously being as clear as possible is required with all communication but it is an absolutely essential part of successful communication in a virtual environment because of factors such as; limited opportunities to obtain clarification, different time-zones, potential language or regional differences, people being situated in different environments and so not able to 'see' what the other person sees (or assumes that the other person knows). With the potential for communication breakdowns being increased, it is more important than ever that things are made clear and nothing is left to assumption or an expectancy of prior knowledge.

Retaining clarity

Every communication should have a purpose. I understand this may sound a bit cold as there is a necessary two way dialogue in human interactions that will include a subtext and will cover all of the other 'conversations' going on such as; 'I like you' and 'you are doing a good job' and so on.

These subtexts are important to consider, but they shouldn't replace the principle objective which is to communicate specific and relevant information from one person to another. From there the niceties can be added, but in our world of countless conversation comebacks (such as; lol, you too, by the way.. etc) we should always make sure that we retain a focus on what the purpose of the communication is, otherwise it will become diluted and after the umpteenth reply you may have both forgotten what you were talking about in the first place.

Sometimes less is more

In my own experience I have found that working remotely in a different time-zone forces me to understand what is expected of me in order that I can get it right first time. My work colleagues are all asleep on the other side of the world and so I cannot just pop my head around the corner of their office and ask for clarification. I have to make sure that I understand and that I am being understood – first time.

However, this has not always been my experience working in a traditional office environment. I have found many times over the years that, because you can always pop your head around the corner of somebody's office, perhaps you don't listen so intently and place the same importance upon understanding it correctly first time. You may have a vague chat which leads to a vague email, of which you may not fully understand. So you set up a meeting with everybody (half of whom may not need to be there, but they'll feel left out if they're not invited to attend) but the actual person who you need to ask for clarification is at another meeting. So you get on with what you believe to be the required work. Upon first review of the work it turns out that it isn't exactly what was required and so you have another meeting (with everybody again) and make sure that the person needed is available to attend this time. You now have a much clearer idea about what is required and are able to begin work - finally.

This is an example of how things are sometimes delayed or compromised due to communication problems. But the problem isn't there because of *insufficient* communication opportunities available; it's there because often there is *too much* availability. There will be five emails sent when one will do, there is a meeting set up when there is not really anything to discuss, there is a briefing session that is not really clearly put together (as the person sits next to you and you can always ask if you've got a problem), and so it goes on.

Consider your medium. Do you really need a video meeting?

I cannot tell you what the best medium will be for all of your various communications, as the content will vary and so the most suitable medium for that particular purpose will also vary. However, I will say that it is important to consider if your choice of medium is a result of you simply looking to replicate the old office environment, and in doing so, carrying over some of the negative and less effective things about it as well.

This is an opportunity to evolve your working practice and develop new ways that are perhaps more streamlined and potentially more effective. A good example of this is in our need to recreate our old 'meetings' in our office life. While it is important to sometimes get together and discuss things collectively, most of us would agree that often times meetings are unproductive, too frequent, not well enough structured and often just an opportunity for the different 'silos' to lock horns. Yet, we continue to book meetings more frequently in the workplace in order to help support the belief that we are being productive and staying busy.

I don't want to disparage all meetings, as it's not the meetings that are the problem but rather their frequency and subsequent level of effectiveness. Too many meetings that are lacking in effectiveness is not something that we should be looking to recreate in the virtual environment.

I've worked on countless projects where I have had to understand the requirements there and then because of the time difference and the deadline involved. Very rarely has a large-scale meeting been appropriate or effective. For my needs email has generally been sufficient, and when very infrequently required then we have used Skype or the phone. Most of the people I have worked with over the years understand the nature of virtual communication and that the need to establish requirements is different to that of a traditional office. Metaphorically speaking a virtual office is like a gun with only one bullet available with which to try and hit the target with first time, whereas a traditional office is like a machine gun that sprays countless bullets in the hope that one or two may hit the target.

I have also experienced other colleagues that have been new to the virtual workplace and have looked to replicate the traditional office conventions by setting up group video meetings for people in different time zones with no real agenda or purpose for the meeting. What would invariably happen in these meetings is that one person would simply read out the email that had already been sent out to everybody which would be followed by awkward silence, with nobody actually understanding what was expected of them. In order to move things along everybody would agree with what was said in the email and say how great it has been to 'catch up' because they actually just want to get on with the work (or evening, depending on what time zone they are on).

Be solution orientated

I know being 'solution orientated' sounds a little like corporate jingo (along with 'singing from the same song-sheet', 'touching base' and 'hitting the ground running' etc) but, believe me, when you shift your attitude and actions in this direction it really makes a big difference to your work and the way that people perceive you.

Being 'solution orientated' simply means being focused on finding a solution, rather than just seeing a problem. A common scenario in the workplace is that an employee has a fixed idea of what their responsibilities are and if something lies outside of these then they will not do it. Often it can physically be done but it is the, 'that's not my job' attitude that prevents this happening.

On occasions there isn't a direct solution and so we have to consider a 'work-around'. Let's imagine that we take our car to two different garages with the same problem. One mechanic says 'It cannot be fixed'. The other one says 'That particular problem cannot be fixed, but I can do this for you instead and it will bring about these results. It will cost this much and I can do it for you on Thursday.' Which one do we go with? Which one do we go back to next time your car has a problem? It's obvious. So, if you apply the same attitude to your own work then you bring about an equally positive reaction in others.

The nature of remote working provides you with an opportunity to shift your orientation towards clarity, focus and taking responsibility through independent action. The results of this positive shift will be evident in your attitude and in your communication.

Form a considered response
If possible, don't reply straight away. Quite often you'll receive a message and have an emotional response to it (good or bad). It's always better to let that emotion simmer before responding, in order that your reply includes more reason than emotion.

One thing I did, when working on a different time zone, was write down my messages in a word document as and when I dealt with each issue. At the end of the day I would read each message back again before sending them one by one. Often I would change a message slightly as I may have learnt something about the issue during my working day, or upon reading it back, and felt it is not quite right having had time to digest it fully.

Become a great writer

The digital world, that we now all live and work in, has brought with it a revival of the written word. You may also be speaking on the phone or via web-video but your main medium of communication will probably be by way of the written word. People cannot see you so cannot make a judgment on your appearance, your accent, your body language or any of the normal things that we base our opinion of somebody on. If your communications are limited to the written word then you need to make sure that you master this skill. Here are some does and don'ts that I have learnt:

- Avoid using CAPS TO EXPRESS YOURSELF. It is seen as aggressive and will potentially bring about confrontation.

- Always read everything back in order to make sure you are happy with it.

- Remember that what you have written cannot be erased. It is 'out there' for anybody to read and you can potentially be forever judged on it.

- Use devices such as bullet points and lists to clarify your message.

Bad Grammar

In this world of quick electronic conversation that is sent on the go, one characteristic that is developing consistently is bad grammar. One misspelt word will say much about the person who has sent that message. It says that they didn't pay enough attention when they wrote the message to make sure they got it right first time but, most of all, it says that they did not care enough about the intended recipient to read it through afterwards.

I understand that being able to spell correctly does not have any bearing on intelligence and that many of the world's most successful entrepreneurs and business titans are dyslexic. But it is less about the ability to spell and more about the discourtesy of not checking and the lack of awareness of the negative impression bad grammar can give.

Most forms of electronic media has a spell-check function which, on the one hand can potentially make us lazy about our ability to spell correctly, but most importantly makes it possible for anybody to communicate using correct grammar. Everybody knows about the spell-check facility being available and so to receive a communication that has not been checked prior to sending gives a poor impression of the person that sent it.

Consider the short attention span that we have all now developed

We are all constantly bombarded with information (in the form of news, spam, advertising, personal communications etc) and it is becoming increasingly hard to keep up with it. As a result we are all developing a much shorter attention span and so it's always a good idea to consider this when you are writing a lengthy message.

Obviously it is best to try and keep the size of the communication to a minimum but you can also make sure that you use plenty of paragraph breaks to make the information more digestible. Also, it is sometimes a good idea to underline or make bold any key points or pertinent points that you want to make. As long as this is used sparingly it will not appear aggressive and it's a good way of making the information easier to take on board. This is especially useful if you need to write an unavoidably long message that has multiple themes within it.

Develop a tone of voice in your 'virtual identity'

In developing a 'tone of voice' in your writing it's important that you sound like you. Make sure that you write in a tone and manner that expresses your personality. How do you do this? Don't think too much about it. Write as you would say it and then read it back to make sure it doesn't break any of the above rules - you don't want to sound like a corporate robot but equally you don't want to sound unprofessional.

There was some interesting research done by Allan Pease and Paul Dunn (for the book 'Write Language') who were curious as to why people wrote letters in an entirely different manner to the way in which they spoke. They suggested that if an individual was to hand a proposal to a business contact in person they would be unlikely to say something like 'Dear John, regarding the conversation that we are having, please find herewith for your perusal documentation as requested by you.' If they spoke to John like that then it would be considered rather strange.

What Pease and Dunne discovered in their research is that letters were written like that because that is how business was discussed in England 200 years ago. This manner of speech has no relation to how the English speaking world articulates today and it is not an easy form of dialogue with which to build rapport in today's modern workplace. Obviously this is directly related to formal letter writing but it is an interesting example of how our way of speaking has evolved in the business world.

So how do you develop a tone of voice in your written word? You should recognise the need to get your personality across and 'speak like you' but always be professional and speak like 'the best version of you.' The key to developing your tone of voice is deciding *what* it is that you want to say as a priority. When you consider *how* you write something as a priority then you're missing the objective of the communication: The message is the content, not the delivery.

Once you have written what you want to 'say' then you can refine the tone of voice, the grammar, the length and structure. It needs to be; professional, sound like you and be clear and to the point. With the art of communication in the virtual workplace the written word is so important and so developing and maintaining the right tone of voice is crucial to get right.

Communicating as part of a team
So we have covered some things about how you, as an individual, can communicate more effectively in a virtual environment. Now let's look at how to interact and collaborate effectively as a part of a virtual team.

What defines a 'team' in a virtual context?

First let us look at defining a 'team' in the virtual context. You are collaborating with others that you may not know well, and perhaps you only see sometimes, or possibly may have never met. This idea of being a 'team' with people that we have no personal relationship with is quite challenging for some of us. So let's look at this.

Our idea of a 'team' is quite often rather simplistic and is often biased towards having a good personal relationship. George Ball; a US Undersecretary of State in JFK's and LBJ's administrations famously said: 'Nothing propinks like propinquity.' By this he meant that nothing fosters a close relationship better than close proximity. Ball popularised this general theme in politics and went on to expand on this idea with what eventually came to be known as the 'Ball Rule of Power' which states that: 'The more direct access you have to the President, the greater your power, no matter what your title actually is.' This is consistent with much of our own thinking about how a team operates. The idea of our removing ourselves from that inner circle and distancing ourselves from the leader (the President) is going against our deeply engrained set of beliefs, but that is the direction that the virtual workplace is taking us and so we need to look to refine our definition of a team, and in particular look at what makes a successful team in this context.

There are many different types of teams but the successful teams are always the ones that recognise a common goal and work towards it together. We see this all the time in sport where, team mates may not necessarily get along personally or even speak the same language, yet they collaborate effectively to work towards their collective objective. We may like to see the team all celebrating their success together and map our own feelings of friendship and camaraderie on to it, but it is the common goal that bonds the team together as opposed to any personal sentiment between individuals.

We do the same with our favourite music bands. We like the idea of them all being great friends and hanging out together after the show. However, this is often not the case and music bands are traditionally made up of very different (and often conflicting) personalities. But they collaborate effectively as a successful team to bring their songs together. That is their shared common goal and that is what creates the bond and the strength in their teamwork.

Over the years I have had many positive relationships with virtual team mates that I have never actually met. It cannot be said that I know them personally as we have not met in person and I know little about their personal lives, but I would consider them to be very good and healthy relationships in the context of the basis that they were formed on. What is this basis? Well, basically to work well together. We have done this very successfully and as a result have formed a mutual appreciation and positive association with one another. Sporting team mates and fellow band members often develop similar positive associations with one another but this relationship is brought about by collaborating effectively and enjoying the resulting success together.

For full-time home based workers the removal of the personal interactions of your former workplace may be missed more by some than others, but it is something that you will need to accept. You will not be in the same physical place as the team mates that will be working alongside you in your work from home initiative (or home based business) and so your interactions with colleagues will, by nature, be less personal. This doesn't have to be seen as a bad thing and by understanding and working towards a common goal of success you will be forming very positive working relationships. If you do miss that personal interaction then it is probably something that you should look to replace or supplement in other areas of your life.

Establish an appropriate level of visibility

Many years ago I worked for a fast-paced company whose projects were often delivered to very tight deadlines and so working late or through the night was commonplace. One particular colleague who worked at the company was not in a department that was called upon to work to these crazy deadlines. He was always known as somebody that was trying to get attention; he was liked, but nobody really took him too seriously as he was always trying a bit too hard to be popular.

One night our team had to work through the night on a deadline and we discovered that this particular colleague had found some reason to be involved on this project. We didn't think too much about it, got the job done, went home for a few hours of sleep and when we got back in to the office we found that he had sent a lengthy 'all-staff' email at 3am telling everybody that we were all working hard, and it was 3am... but we were doing well, and it was 3am... and our company is great, and it was 3am... and so it went on. Unfortunately his attempt to draw positive attention to himself resulted in the opposite reaction and the '3am email' was certainly noticed, but for all the wrong reasons.

When you are working as a part of a virtual team you will find that it's important to strike a balance in the frequency of your communication. You don't want to be contacting people endlessly (because perhaps you're feeling lonely and miss the office water cooler chats) and distracting them from getting on with their work. Equally you don't want to become distant and uncommunicative to the point that nobody knows what you are up to and how things are going for you. This is particularly true for flexible workers where you need to maintain a good level of communication during your time spent working at home. If you are known for going 'off the grid' on your working from home days then it is possible that this will generate some resentment and make things difficult for your colleagues.

Consider how you will potentially be perceived by your communications

Just as you will put together a perception of your virtual colleagues, they will be forming a perception of you. These impressions will have been pieced together by each communication that you will have shared, and will include many of the things that we have covered in this section about communication. Will you be seen as professional? Will you be seen as a bit over-bearing and needy? Will you be seen as abrupt and perhaps rude?

In the same way as when we read a book, we piece

together a picture of each character in our minds; we do the same with our virtual relationships. The picture that we develop is not always accurate and is often formed very early on. After a short time in the story we will form an image of that person because some of the early prompts caused you to make that connection and form that mental image. So, it's worth understanding that, just as in off-line communications, our impressions will be formed (and often indelibly set) very early on.

Communicating throughout different regions
In this global workplace that many of us now inhabit it is common to be operating as part of a team of individuals that are distributed globally. Let's take a look a look at this:

Regional language
Obviously we are all now working in a global workplace and so many of people will come in to regular contact with people who speak their language as a second tongue. Those of us that are fortunate enough to speak English as a first language often take this for granted and have little awareness of the challenges that others (whose first language is not English) may face in communicating accurately and effectively. This is not news to us but it is something to always be aware of. If a communication is misleading or confusing in some way then it is worth seeking clarification on, rather than being critical or looking to discriminate for their lack of perfection in a second tongue.

Cultural differences
There are countless examples of cultural difference all around the world, and far too many for the scope of this

book to address but the relevant point here is that they exist. Be aware of potential differences, consider how they may be a factor in your global communication and perhaps learn about them to further your own understanding.

Local dialect and colloquialisms
It is important to be aware of the use of local dialect and colloquialisms in your communication. Every area in every country has an array of colloquialisms that will be well known locally. They will also often have their own dialect in their particular way of phrasing something. Outside of that area these ways of communicating will be unknown, of little use and potentially confusing. There will be countless examples of this around the world and, again, it's worth being aware of these and not using phrases that others may not understand.

Different grammar and phraseology
Perhaps the more tricky area is in the grammar and phraseology that you use every day and are not aware that others may not understand it. An example of this is here in Australia, people often begin a sentence by saying 'Look, I think...' this is quite normal and acceptable but where I originate from in the UK to start a sentence like this would be considered quite aggressive and the only time you would do it is when you are strongly and firmly looking to make your point.

In Australia the word 'look' is added to start of most sentences when somebody is expressing some sort of idea or opinion. In the UK you would only use that word at the start of a sentence if you became exasperated and the person you were talking to really didn't understand you. You would probably do this with a raised voice, expressing impatience and a degree of hostility. This is an example that I have had to be aware of in the years that I have been living and working in Australia but for a UK employer. This is just a single word that can potentially cause such confusion between two countries that both speak the same language.

Time differences
This sounds pretty obvious but it is important that you are aware of the recipient's time zone so that you can form appropriate expectations on their response. If it is the middle of the night for them and they are asleep then clearly you are not going to get a reply straight away, no matter how many CAPS you use in your email.

Our virtual team
So now let's look at putting it all together with an example of a message being communicated within a hypothetical 'virtual' team. They are entirely fictitious characters that are required to collaborate together in a virtual context.

These are communications from different people that are following up on work that 'John' is currently doing for them. Let's get ourselves introduced to the team members, read their emails to John and see if we can answer the questions at the end of it:

Janice:
She has been with the company forever. She complains about it, but everybody knows that she loves it. She refers to everybody as 'the gang'. She is the event

organiser, the centre of gossip and the font of all knowledge. She wants to be liked, and to like others.

Janice's message to John reads:

Hi John,
Hope you had a good weekend? We had a family barbeque, which was great but the weather was terrible. As usual, the weekend flew by too quickly ☹
Never mind, I've got a nice holiday to look forward to in a few weeks ☺

It'd be good if you could get that work over to me as soon as it's ready.

Have a great day

Janice

Steve:

Steve is a go-getter and likes to think of himself as such. He has a tangible idea of success and likes to talk about his little victories. He drives a car to express his status and likes to impress his personality upon others.

Steve's message to John reads:

John,
I'm waiting for that work you're doing for me. Can you get it over to me asap?

Toby:

Toby has been at the company for as long as anybody can remember and started out as a junior. He does a bit of everything and can lay his hand to many different skills. He is an invaluable person to have around. He will always work late if required. He is quiet and shy but happy in himself and confident in his abilities. He can fix anything and enjoys doing so.

Toby's message to John reads:

Hi John,
If you could let me have that work as soon as possible that'd be great, because Dave has been asking me about it

Thanks

Toby

Justine:

Justine is always the last to leave at night and often works at weekends. She loves her work but feels she has a point to prove and is sensitive about potentially being overlooked. She is very intelligent; she has good education and good client skills. She is ambitious and expects everybody else to share her ambitions. She will plan her working calendar as a seven day week and will expect others to be available at those times too.

Justine's message to John reads:

Hi John,

I'm just checking on the progress of that work that you're doing for me. I told Dave that he could have it on Monday, so I'll be in at the weekend again. If you could get it to me before the weekend so that I can proof-read it on Saturday and get the amends back for you to do on Sunday (sorry, hope you didn't have any plans, but this is an important project ;)

Please give me a call on my mobile if you have any problems.

You're a star. I owe you one.

Justine

Jake:
Jake is young and likes to think of himself as still at University. He keeps to himself and doesn't want to socialise with the 'old' people at work. He is very smart and good at his job but is lacking in communication skills. Jake is a little too ego-centric and doesn't 'get' why he has to communicate things onwards, as he considers this to be 'checking up' on him.

He didn't send a message to John

Here are some questions about these messages:

What is the purpose of the communication?
The purpose of each email probably came across as being varied. They were all requesting a progress update from John but not everybody actually asked for a response on John's progress. The subtext of some of the emails came over as the principle message, with Janice trying to make sure that John liked her and Steve being intent on letting John know that he was an important person. Other emails did not have such overt subtexts but still only conveyed the perspective of the sender; Toby's email said that Dave had been asking him about the work (Dave always sees Toby as his 'go-to' guy) and Justine had planned to get the work to Dave early, and work over the weekend to make this happen (and by making this decision, she had also committed John to work over the weekend too.)

When is the project's actual deadline?
None of the emails actually stated when the project's specific deadline was. They were all vague on dates except Justine but she only said when she had told Dave he would see the work, she didn't specify what the actual deadline was.

What actual deliverables are expected from John?
None of the emails specified the deliverables that were expected.

Would you consider them to be positive interactions between John and his team mates?
Each email was representative of the person's character that had sent it and would each potentially create a

different reaction from John towards his different co-workers. He may feel overwhelmed and confused by Janice, he is likely to be annoyed by Steve, not much about Toby, bullied by Justine and he would feel particularly resentful towards Jake if his lack of communication resulted in a problem with the project's delivery and John receiving the blame.

A positive communication that covers the points we have made may be something like the following:

Hi John,
I'm just checking on the progress of the work that we are doing for Dave.

Just to confirm that I need **4 gizmos** and that the deadline to get these over to Dave is 2:00 Tuesday 14 May. If you could please make sure you get these to me **by 12:00 on Monday**, as that'll give me time to proof read them on Monday afternoon and get any **amends** back for you to do on Tuesday morning before final checks and then sending them on to Dave.

If you could just drop me a line back to **confirm** that these timings are ok for you I'd appreciate it. As ever, please give me a call anytime if you have any problems.

Many thanks

Amanda

The purpose of the communication is clearly stated.

The project's actual deadline is clear with a proposed plan of how they could both work together to meet their deadline, plus a request to confirm if that was acceptable to John.

The deliverables are clearly indicated.

John is likely to feel positive about this communication with Amanda as he has been made aware of what is expected of him. He is also likely to feel that Amanda is collaborating well with him so that they can work together to bring about a positive resolution to this project — many of the other emails suggest that John works for the person that sent them, as they talk about the work that John is doing for them.

4. IMPROVE YOUR WORK-LIFE BALANCE

'It's long been my opinion that the best thing you can do for the world, is the best thing you can do for you. Make out your 'want list' because it is by getting what you want that you will make your biggest contribution to society. We do that which we are motivated to do; the greater the motivation, the more we do. We are motivated most not by what we think we should be doing most for the world, rather from what we most want from the world'

Earl Nightingale

The above quotation from Earl Nightingale is the foundation for this next chapter where we look at 'what is in it for you.' The main theme of the quote being that we do our best for others by being adequately motivated by our own needs. Translated in to this context by saying that we make the best contribution in our professional lives if working from home benefits our own personal lives. The opportunity to work from home carries with it the potential to really change *your life* for the better, so let's look at how you can do that.

What is 'work-life balance'?

The signature benefit of working from home is the ability to achieve an improved work-life balance. But what is 'work-life balance' and what does it look like in terms of your own individual set of circumstances? The idea of a good work-life balance has become something of a cliché. It is one of the hot topics of contemporary living and sits alongside other lifestyle clichés such as 'financial freedom' and 'optimum health.' These are important parts of modern life that we would all do well to explore for ourselves, but they have unfortunately become clichés that we perhaps don't take seriously anymore because of our over-exposure to them.

These are the great 'white elephants' that we are all seeking and there are huge industries that have been created to fuel our desires for these mythical states of contemporary bliss. The media images that drive our desires are of older couples that have reached the Valhalla of *financial freedom*. We see middle aged people that enjoy such a wonderful *work-life balance* that they are home working with their child happily sitting on their lap. We see all age groups in gym clothes, sipping at health drinks and living life to the full due to their *optimum health*.

These images, and the ideas that support them, have become so commonplace that they have lost their validity to many of us. Whenever anybody mentions the latest health trend, we cannot help but feel skeptical because of the countless fads that have preceded them. Whenever anyone introduces us to the latest way to achieve financial freedom, we cannot help but feel cynical and our reaction is often 'Ok, how much is this financial freedom going to cost me?' It is the same for work-life balance. Do we really believe that there is such a thing or is this just another urban myth that is simply a part of a booming health and wellness industry?

Let's look at some statistics:
- More than 10% of Australian male employees work more than 11 hours a day.

- 85% Australian employees felt life was becoming and had become more frantic.

- 85% of Americans say they want more time with their family and 46% say they want 'much more'. In the UK, 36% say they want 'much more' time with their families.

- A recent survey of Australian fathers found that 68% felt they did not spend enough time with their children. 60% attributed this to 'barriers in the workplace' (such as expectations of long working hours and inflexibility).

- When it comes to the imbalance between work and family life, surprisingly Australia ranks at the bottom of the entire developed world.

- The Australian Bureau of Statistics tells a similar grim story. Australians, on average, spend 50 hours a week at work – and that's not taking into account the time spent responding to emails and making work calls after hours.

Although we can always make statistics support any predetermined point of view, these figures do appear to paint a pretty bleak picture of an increasingly demanding work culture.

So let's now look at the opportunity available to you and consider what a good work-life balance actually looks like.

What is a good work-life balance in reality?
In order to see if a good work-life balance is achievable let's first define exactly what it is.

A good work-life balance is a positive and healthily weighted application of your time and efforts in both your professional life and your personal life. That's it. It is not to have everything. It is to have a well-proportioned combination of some things; not a totally bulging package of everything. Having everything is not the objective of establishing *balance* and it's also not possible, as there are always sparkly new things being introduced that we could add to our list of essentials.

The important part of establishing if we can ever achieve it is to first define what 'it' is – for you. If you are taking advantage of a flexible working arrangement with your employer and are working one day a week from home, then you can focus your intention on how that particular day can be made special and how you can make best use of the extra time that you will have available. If you are working from home on a part-time basis for practical reasons (caring for a family member for example) then the challenges will be different but the opportunity has great potential on a practical and emotional level. If your work duties are carried out at home (small business start-ups, independent sales consultant etc) then the need to balance your dual commitments will be crucial in your ability to achieve your potential success. If you are switching to a full-time work from home arrangement (by choice or by necessity) then you perhaps face the biggest challenges in terms of the changes taking place, but you also have the biggest opportunity in terms of potential for lifestyle change. Whatever your individual set of circumstances the ability to work from home gives you the potential to improve your overall work-life balance.

So how do you want to improve your work-life balance? What goals do you want to set that will result in meeting your objectives? The important part about setting goals is to define achievable goals; otherwise they no longer serve as a motivation to strive for but rather a stick to beat ourselves with: 'I'm still not earning enough. I'm still not slim enough. I still don't have enough time etc.' And we live in a world that constantly raises the bar on the expectations that we place upon ourselves. Women have to be beautiful, thin, have a successful career and be a perfect mother. Men have to fit, handsome, successful at work but also doting fathers and husbands with time available - and flowers in their hands.

These are not *all* possible, not just because we're not all slim and gorgeous, but because if you want uber-success at work then you will have less time at home. If you want to be the perfect mother then you will have less time available to invest in a successful career. And yet we are all trying to aspire to these completely unattainable goals, which often no longer inspire us but serve as those sticks used to beat ourselves with. Remember, the aim is to have a good balance of things in your lolly bag. Not the whole shop.

Why is balance so hard to find?
Nature is all about balance. We're surrounded by things in the natural world that all adhere to a natural order of balance. So why is it so hard to find this balance in our lives?

Yes, nature is good at balance but we're not. If you look at anything that is governed by human sentiment and emotion then it tends to swing from one extreme end of the spectrum to the other. Politics, religion, economics; yes, there are happy mediums in there but the overall trend is often with the pendulum swinging to its full extent before giving way to its natural inclination to reverse that force.

Even though it goes through a middle ground it seldom stops in a place that we are happy with. It'll keep going until we reach the other end of the scale and we experience enough discomfort to once again make a change. We see this with political parties from the right being voted in as a consequence of everybody being frustrated with the left party; and then it reverses again a number of years later.

We are also not very good at achieving balance because it has not ranked highly on our priority list. We have never really been big on identifying balance as a goal. In man's long history of conquest we have seldom sought a balance with the native people that we are conquering but rather domination.

So, for one reason or another we humans are not very good at finding balance. But it's also not easy to know when something is *in balance*. On an undetermined journey it is not easy to pick where the half-way point will be.

In hindsight we can often see when we should have stopped hunting that animal that is now extinct. We can look back at charts of a stock to see *when* we should have sold, before it bombed and we lost out. The history books show us exactly what point a political dictator gained their critical mass and it was no longer possible for individuals to say no to them.

How do we measure our work-life balance?
So if it's that hard to identify, then how do we know when we've found it? How do we know what success looks like in this area of our lives? You don't ever really know. You feel it. You feel better about yourself, about your relationships, about your health, and so on. But it's never a fixed point of success but an on-going journey. There are constant tweaks and applications and it is simply a work in progress.

In the same way, our work-life balance is a headline grabbing measurement that everybody wants to know; 'Have you got balance or not?' But it is not as simple as that. It is made up of endless amounts of underlying balances between our time and commitments that are constantly being played out in our individual lives:

Parenthood <=> Career
Spending money <=> Saving money
Eating the food you enjoy <=> Eating healthy food
Treating your kids <=> Disciplining your kids
Backing yourself individually <=> Being a team player
Playing sport <=> Watching sport
Saving money <=> Investing money
Focusing on your strengths <=> Diversifying your skills

The rich man will always want more time and the idle man will always want more money, but for the rest of us (who are somewhere in the middle) it is a constant juggle between how much we value our; time, money, careers, professional identity, role as a parent, health, enjoyment, education, and so on.

What does a good work-life balance look like?
There is no one-size-fits-all solution for a good work-life balance. It will be something that is unique to you and your own set of circumstances. For me personally working from home has enabled me the opportunity to spend time with my family during the early years of their growing up, and to share in all of the little experiences that I would have otherwise missed. It has given me the precious gift of time and I have used that time to fulfill my own ambitions in ways that I would have otherwise been unable to do.

Without my journey to and from work I found myself with an extra four hours available to me every day. That's nearly 1000 hours per year and (if you divide that in to 12 hour days) that's an extra 83 days per year.

Within that time I have been available to go to my kid's

school assemblies, help them with their homework, go to the park or play in the garden. I have built go-karts and tree-houses with them, started businesses with my wife, always been my son's soccer coach, trained for and run marathons, learnt many new skills, renovated houses and I have written this book. These extra hours have enabled me to be there at meal-times, to read bed-time stories to my kids, to know all of their friends and to share in their lives and have a good understanding and empathy with the various things going on in their lives. I have helped all my kids learn to ride their bikes and I have been there to share in all of their achievements, as they accomplish new and exciting things themselves.

Lifestyle innovation

Personally, I have absolutely no doubt that history will record the present time as a 'digital revolution' to match that of the industrial revolution in the way that it has changed the world that we live in so fundamentally. This era of innovation is bringing about such significant changes in the way we work and communicate and it is also bringing the bi-product of *'lifestyle innovation'*.

As with many innovations, it is often the bi-products that really catch on; texting was added to mobile phones just because it was there. The developers considered that nobody would use it; why would people type a message when they could speak to someone instead? How glad they were that they included the ability to text. In a similar way; the digital infrastructure of modern office life was not set up to enable the ability to work remotely, but it has become a very positive and welcome bi-product of it.

What does a good work-life balance look like to you?
The statistics that we looked at earlier showed that many of us are saying 'yes, we'd like more time.' As we said earlier, time in itself has no intrinsic value; it's what we do with that time that gives it any sense of meaning or definition. You now have the potential opportunity of more time. So, what will you choose to do with it?

Let's start considering that question of 'What does a good work-life balance look like to you?

Your own individual circumstances
It's not a competition and there is no right or wrong answer. As we said in the introduction, this book should be used as a blue-print with which to map your own experiences and set of circumstances on to. Everybody's situation will be different and will also change as time goes by. When we're in our twenties we go to a lot of weddings. When we're in our thirties we got to a lot of christenings and children's parties. When we are in our forties many of us are made redundant from our middle-management positions, are needed less by our kids and start to reevaluate our lives. And so it goes on. These are obviously sweeping generalisations, but they are examples of stages that we go through in our lives and these stages will be reflected in our lives outside of the workplace – those lives that we will be embedding our working lives into when we work from home.

Let's look at kids for example. It may be that you are at the stage where you are desperate to see more of your young kids, and they are at an age where they will really benefit from your being there. It may be that your kids are older and more independent and simply don't need you there as much. It may be that you feel the best way that you can look after your kids is to be a good provider, and have perhaps never been a 'kiddy' person who likes to play and act silly. You're happy with being able to provide well for them, and spend time with them at the weekends.

What about relationships? Are you in a relationship and, if so, is it a good one? Would you want to spend more time with your partner? If yes, then great you can. If no, then; could your relationship benefit from having more time available for one another? It is a stereo-typed scenario in modern day life where two people get together because they like each other but then the all-consuming needs of raising a family become such that they lose touch and their relationship becomes increasingly distant. As I say, it is a stereo-type but it is a common situation nonetheless. Is this you? Could you benefit from reconnecting with the person that you once decided to share your life with? Maybe you and your partner are happy with things as they are. You are committed to your work and they are committed to their own work or their interests, and neither wants to involve the other. It's a common situation of days gone by that a retired man would get under his wife's feet, because she's not used to having him around and he doesn't know what to do with himself now. Is this you?

What about ambition and lifestyle? Do you have a burning ambition that you've not been able to pursue as you've not had time due to work commitments? You may be able to pursue it now with the extra time you'll have. Do you have a hobby that you're looking forward to being able to spend more time doing? Is there an image of a lifestyle that you'd like to try and achieve for yourself? Even if you are only working from home one day a week, that is still extra time available and the potential opportunity to do something that you could not do before.

Blank canvas
Whenever we're put on the spot and asked to think of something, then it adds increased pressure and our minds go blank. When you haven't spoken to someone for a while and they ask 'What have you been up to?' You may have been to Timbuktu, crossed the Andes or won an Olympic gold medal, but your mind will still go blank and you'll reply 'Oh, not much; the usual.'

When you are presented with a blank piece of paper and told to draw anything you like; you cannot think of anything. When you go to a book shop or library and there is so much choice that your mind goes blank as to where to start. In order to paint this picture of how we want to change our lives, we first need to decide what it is that we want to paint. Spend some time considering what you want in your picture. Think about some of the things that we have discussed and brain-storm it. Discuss it with your partner and why not deploy some 'blue sky' thinking.

Referring back to our Earl Nightingale quote again:
'Make out your 'want list' because it is by getting what you want that you will make your biggest contribution to society.'

Create a 'want-list'

What would be on your want-list? If you can picture it clearly enough then you're one step closer to making it happen. I don't mean the 'think it and it'll happen' coffee-table psychology. I mean that if you create a strong enough vision of something in your mind, then you can then start drawing up a clear plan of how you can bring this about. Look at it as if it were your dream home that you were building; if you knew exactly what it looked like in your mind, then you can draw up clear and concise blue-prints that would make actually building the house so much easier and more achievable. Alternatively, if you only have a few vague ideas of a house and draw up a number of different sets of plans (all equally vague), then that house is never likely to be your dream home, if it ever gets built at all. It's the same process with building anything and, the first stage of creating a reality is to develop a vision.

The cycle of satisfaction

A situation often occurs in the workplace where we become unhappy with our current job and find a reason to attach to it: 'My boss doesn't appreciate me' or 'They don't pay me enough' or any number of other reasons. We then move to another organisation and are happy for a while but then after a short time this job also breeds dissatisfaction for the same or similar reasons; and so the cycle goes on. How many of us have either done this ourselves or witnessed it in others? This is a common pattern within the workplace that indicates that the dissatisfaction felt by the individual lies within them, and they simply *map* the cause of it on to some external thing in their working environment.

When you realise the potential of enjoying an improved work-life balance not only will you be motivated to maintain it, but that improved state of well-being will also help you to go from strength to strength and improve your potential to achieve increased professional success. The positive forces feed off of each other to help propel you forward.

With your improved attitude towards your working life you will be able to create a 'cycle of satisfaction.' This is consistent with research that demonstrates how organisations that offer flexible and remote working opportunities very often record improved standards of performance and high staff retention levels as a result.

The alignment of interests

This chapter has all been about you. What's in it for you. But if you use this personal motivation towards achieving your own success then this in turn benefits your organisation. By creating a better work-life balance for yourself and achieving professional success you will be positively contributing to the overall success of your organisation.

There is no better way of harnessing a collective of individuals than to have them share a collective goal. Each individual's 'why' is multiplied to produce a powerful compound effect that will drive everybody together in the same direction and be jointly motivated and rewarded with the ensuing success.

The *challenge* of working from home is to successfully transfer your working practice to the home working environment. But the *opportunity* is so much more.

5. IMPLEMENT SUSTAINABLE AND LASTING CHANGES

'A mind that is stretched by a new experience can never go back to its old dimensions'
Oliver Wendell Holmes, Jr

Over the course of this book we've looked at things that you can do to improve your effectiveness in working from home, and you have now started to consider what an improved work-life balance potentially looks like for you. Now let's look at making the required changes to bring about improvement in our personal and professional lives, and also how we make these changes sustainable and lasting. To do that we need to first look at how we implement new behaviour and how our brain works in managing change.

Understanding our brain and its role in dealing with change

Over the last two decades there have been huge discoveries in understanding how our brain works. In fact, neuroscientists have estimated that 98% of everything that we know about how our brains work has been discovered in the last decade. This is largely due to our developing technology that now enables us to scan the human brain in real-time, and so study exactly how things work. These advances in research not only represent a huge increase in our potential to discover so much more, but they have also led scientists to estimate that over 80% of what we thought we knew about how the brain works has actually turned out to be incorrect.

So, how does this help us? Well, by understanding how our brains process new information, we are developing a better understanding of how we deal with and manage change. While we're talking about change (as a set of external information to be processed) it's worth considering that, just like the rest of our body, the physical parts of our brain are made up of cells that are constantly dying off and being replaced. As such, our brains are in a constant state of flux and, every second, about 10 million cells are dying off and being replaced. With an on-going decommissioning and renewing of countless numbers of cells our brains are constantly changing and forging new neural connections, to the degree that; if you were to write out the number of possible neural connections your brain can make, it would take you 75 years just to write out all of the zeros!

Mind boggling stuff I'm sure you'll agree, but let's now look more specifically at the role our amazing brains play in managing change.

Our brains are made up of eight key areas: frontal lobe, motor cortex, parietal lobe, occipital lobe, cerebellum, 'gatekeeper,' temporal lobe and the prefrontal cortex, but the brain essentially operates with two main parts;

the conscious and the non-conscious.

Conscious brain

The conscious part of our brain is the 'captain of the ship.' It is responsible for our thinking, our reasoning and in exercising our freewill. This is the part of the brain that will consider options and make new decisions. However, for all of its power in making our decisions, the conscious part of our brain only has a limited say in what we actually *do*.

The main limitation of the conscious part of our brain is its attention span. It comes up with all of our ideas and is very much the place where our dreams and visions are formed, but they just don't last long. The conscious brain is all about dealing with new information and new ideas, but its processing power is limited, as it is on to the next idea by then. Research shows that the average person loses focus every 6 to 10 seconds, as this is their conscious part of the brain.

Non-conscious brain

The non-conscious part of the brain takes care of all of the things that we do not have to think about. It assumes control of the running of our bodies, and it is a good job too because if it was left to our conscious brains we wouldn't last any more than 6 seconds before it lost focus on what it was doing.

How we can make significant and sustainable change

We can make change with our conscious brain, but it is by deploying our non-conscious brain that we make the changes sustainable, and we do this by changing our habits. The non-conscious part of our brain is where all of our learning (memory) is stored and, importantly, where our habits reside.

According to research more than 90% of our daily actions are habitual and are carried out without conscious thought. You will implement lasting change in your reality if you make a change in your habits. If you rely on thinking 'Oh, I need to do this...' then it will never become a lasting and deeply rooted change. This is exactly why people join a gym in January but then their good intentions are forgotten about by March; because the conscious brain made the decision to join the gym, but then moved on to dealing with other things. The realisation of the dream of improved fitness will be a combination of the conscious brain making the important decision to join the gym, and the non-conscious brain taking over to form the new habits of behaviour that will result in the person showing up at the gym, without having to think about it.

However, creating habits is more complex than simply doing things 'without thinking'; to be more precise, it is doing things *instinctively* and not as a response to (and having to wait for) conscious thought to have taken place first.

Have you ever driven home, pulled in to your drive way and had no recollection of the journey that you have just taken? How on earth did you get there without killing yourself? You took the journey home, with all of its numerous life-threatening decisions, not without *thinking* but rather without *conscious thinking*.

How do we develop new positive ways of behaviour?

So how do we make sure that our conscious brain is passing over all of the relevant information to our non-conscious brain, which is then assuming control and forming new habits?

Basically, things become learnt by the non-conscious brain by being repeated over and over again. We were only able to make that car journey safely because we have driven a car so many times that it has become learnt as a habit. We need our conscious part of the brain (us) to be aware that repetition is required in order for things to develop in to habits. Consistency in our conscious actions and behaviours will eventually bring about our being able to repeat the process without having to consciously think about it.

Habits, beliefs and reality

When you think something over and over it becomes a habit of thought. When you repeat a habit of thought over and over it eventually becomes a belief. A 'belief' is simply a deeply embedded habit that has formed within you and has become so deeply rooted that it now contributes to a part of your overall personality or 'belief system.' When more than one person shares the same belief it can potentially become stronger and sharing in a 'mass belief' can result in something so strongly defined that it can often move on from being a 'belief' to a perceived reality.

If we are saying that reality is a certain perception that we all collectively share and subscribe to, then there are countless examples of this in everyday society. Traffic lights, for example, do not force you to stop when they turn red, but rather it is the social conditioning that we all share that enforces this action within each individual. With each individual contributing consistently it brings about a reality that all cars stop at a red light. So, given this as an example it is not the traffic light that has the power but the collective attitudes, habits and social behaviour that has the power.

This is an example of something that we learn to do with our conscious brain (we stop at red when we are learning to drive), and then do instinctively with repetition (by our non-conscious brain). This habit is shared by others to the point where it has become a 'belief', and this commonly agreed belief has come to be perceived as a 'reality', that all cars stop at red lights.

If the rules were suddenly changed and the red light meant go and the green light meant stop then it would not be easy to suddenly 'unlearn' such deeply rooted habits and behaviours. In much the same way, we all have a shared belief that a workplace is where you go to work. This belief could be considered a perceived reality and it may be hard for some us to unlearn that; in the same way as going on red may be difficult to unlearn. But sometimes change we must; and it helps to retrace how certain ideas have been adopted and have gained their power and their significance, in order that we can create new 'realities'.

You may have heard the story about the elephant that is tied only with an old piece of rope and stick in the ground. The fully grown elephant could easily pull themselves free from this bond but, as a baby elephant it tried to do just that and couldn't, and so it learnt that the bond couldn't be moved and set its behaviour accordingly. Now the thing that keeps the elephant bound is not the reality of the situation but rather their own deeply engrained belief and subsequent behaviour that has defined and created their own reality.

We all have established ideas of 'who we are', 'what we do' and 'where we do it.' But it's interesting to see where these ideas have been derived from. They start as an idea, then become a habit of behaviour, then they become a belief, until finally they are considered to be a reality.

By retracing the process and understanding how ideas have become deeply engrained ways of behaviour, we can see how we can proactively go about creating new ways of behaviour that help us to adapt and succeed in our changing world.

Nothing comes from nothing
It's really important to understand that the ability to work from home does not bring about a better work-life balance, in itself. It simply provides you with the *opportunity* to create one.

Whatever your own work-life balance is destined to be (good or bad), it will be the product of a combination of the changes that you make. If you do not make any changes then nothing will change. This isn't a competition to see who can make the most of the opportunity of working from home, but if you want to maximise the opportunity but do not instigate any change then nothing will change. Nothing comes from nothing, and it's crucial to recognize that.

So how do we go about making the required changes to enable us to work more effectively from home, and to enjoy a better work-life balance?

Step 1: Form an intention

Earl Nightingale, who we were introduced to in the previous chapter, has another great quote that explains his belief that people only do what they form an intention to do. He said, 'People do what they make up their minds to do.' He then goes on to explain this further by saying: 'You see, a woman who does not think about baking an apple pie for dinner tonight will never think of looking up the recipe for apple pie. Without the decision for pie there is no motivation for checking out the recipe.'

Nothing will happen without you first *forming an intention* of what it is that you wish to make happen.

Here is a question: There were 5 people in a boat and one decided to jump in the water for a swim. How many people are now in the boat?

There are still 5 people. One only *decided* to jump. He didn't yet move. He had established an intention but without the required action then he remains in the boat.

Step 2: Take the required action

This is much like our earlier example of *deciding* that we are going to get fit and join a gym in January. Joining the gym and having the intention of getting fit does not produce the required results. It is a good start but it is only by taking *action* and going to the gym that we will get fit.

You can hypothesise and speculate on an outcome as much as you like but unless you take action then nothing will ever happen, and you will never know what might have been. We pretty much all know this to be true, but it is surprising how often we don't commit to taking the action required for the things that we say we want. Many of us will buy a book or watch a TV show and be really inspired and motivated by it. 'Ok, that's it. I'm going to change my life', we say. What happens next? The passion and emotional charge begins to fade and those little voices of doubt start whispering.

As well as the doubts what else happens at this stage? Remember how we learnt about the short attention span of our conscious mind and how only 'thinking' about change is short-lived due to the nature of the conscious brain? This is what happens here; we're fired up about the idea, but then that excitement and emotion starts to fade as the conscious mind loses its focus and moves on to something else. So the final thing we need do to create lasting and sustainable change is to repeatedly and consistently commit to taking the actions required, in order that they become subconscious habits in our behavior.

Step 3: Change your habits
Remember, more than 90% of our daily actions are habitual and are carried out without conscious thought. You will implement lasting change in your reality if you make a change in your habits of behaviour.

By working from home everybody has the opportunity to improve their overall professional performance and their work-life balance. However, the ones that go on to improve their lives will be the ones that make it their intention to make change, put the relevant actions in place to bring about that change, and then turn those actions in to consistent habits of behaviour.

Let's look at this in a realistic scenario
If you have two extra hours available each day, with no travel time to work, then you have an extra two hours available to you. You need to recognize that, and take note of the significance of it and the possibilities available. If you don't, then the chances are that you will simply use this time pottering around on Facebook or 'checking your emails' then guess what? You will not be using this time to effect change.

If you *want* to do this with the extra time that you have then that is fine, but you need to understand that by 'checking emails' you will be starting work and therefore surrendering the extra time that you have been presented with. That is your choice and you need to take responsibility for that decision, but you will be missing the opportunity to implement positive changes and make this a beneficial change for you.

Let's look at some of the ingredients of an improved work-life balance.

Opportunity for improved health
How can working from home improve your health? In itself it can't; after all you will still be carrying out the

same duties as before. What it does give you is the additional time and a new environment to be able to pursue better health and, as we have said, what you choose to do with this time is up to you. Instead of the commute into work each morning and evening you could go for a run, go to the gym or have a swim. You could walk the dog, take the kids to the park or go for a bike ride with your partner.

It also gives you the opportunity to use your lunch break effectively – after all you've probably spent all morning sitting down, why not take the opportunity to move your limbs and get your heart pumping? You could take some exercise in your lunch break, instead of going to the shops or sitting around chatting with your colleagues.

It also gives you a working environment that you do not have to share with others. You can therefore listen to music that makes you feel happy in your work or inspires you. You can learn new ways to improve your health, such as yoga, pilates or many others. Whereas before you would be limited to going to the gym in the evenings or at weekends, you can now easily add healthy activities to your daily routine. You can replace coffee breaks in the office with taking short breaks from your home-office to dedicate to improving your health.

You can try new things without having to discuss it or feel the need to justify them to your colleagues. You can try a new diet, without having to talk about it all the time and feel pressured to present visible results in weight-loss. You can learn to meditate and add meditation to your daily working routine, without having to sit in the middle of a busy office 'omming'.

There are ever increasing amounts of new research in the area of health and lifestyle that you can explore for yourself. For example, as well as the seemingly endless new-fad diets that are being introduced to us, there are also new developments such as the health implications of sitting all day. There is growing evidence that the huge amounts of time that we all spend sitting down is becoming increasingly detrimental to our health, and many people are subscribers to the belief that 'sitting is the new smoking.' If this was something that you wanted to explore for yourself then there is no reason that you couldn't remove your chair, raise your desk and experiment with standing up and working.

I'm not suggesting that you should do this but, with your home-office being solely for your use, this is a good example of something that you would have the opportunity to do for yourself – where before, it just may not have been possible. You could try it for a period of time and if you liked it then you could continue the practice and, if not, you could revert back to your chair. Not a big deal, not a problem. In order to do this in your old office you may have had to either (1) put the idea to your boss who would potentially consult with HR and then apply for the budget for new desks for everybody. The decision of enforcing this on others would be yours and the responsibility of its success or failure would be yours also. Alternatively (2) You could just do it yourself and perhaps feel a bit self-conscious standing up in an office where everybody else was sitting down. You'd have to endure endless chats about whether the benefits were showing or not and, ultimately, if you ended up sitting down again you would feel as self-conscious as you did when you were standing up. This is a scenario that may never happen in reality because the hassle involved and the potential derision would be a big enough barrier for most of us to never pursue it.

It's probably also worth noting here while we're talking about health that our continued advancement with technology brings with it increased automation and less physical human activity. The simple fact is that many of us physically move less for our work nowadays and we look to replace that physical activity by things such as going to the gym. Working from home continues this trend with cutting out the need to travel in to our workplace. Even if we were driving or sitting on a train, it is likely that there will have been more physical effort involved previously when we had to physically get from A to B. It's worth recognising that now we're working from home we're not even required to do that anymore and so we're increasing the potential need to replace this physical activity in some way.

Opportunity for better relationships

There is no doubt that marriages and personal relationships are very often casualties in our struggle with the demands on modern life, but these struggles and time limitations can also often be used as an excuse and something to hide behind.

With more time available for your personal relationships you will have the opportunity to give your loved ones more time. What you choose to do with this additional time is up to you.

Opportunity for better lifestyle

You have the opportunity to work from home and that can give you the launch-pad to fundamentally improve your working life, and with it your health, relationships and so much more.

You may want to take this opportunity to broaden your mind and open yourself up to new ideas that you may not have considered before. There are not only new things to learn about the 'working' component of this change but there are also lots of things that you can learn about the 'living' side of the equation. There is a whole wealth of inventory available for self-development that you are able to explore.

This is the perfect opportunity for you to be able to implement significant and meaningful changes to your lifestyle. It may be a new hobby, more time for an existing one, learning a new language or anything on that 'I never get time for' list. Change is here already, so why not do whatever you can to make it a change for the better?

SUMMARY

'Life can only be understood backwards;
but it must be lived forwards'
Soren Kierkegaard

The ability to work from home can provide many potential benefits for individuals and for organisations.

For individuals those potential benefits include; greater opportunities for professional success through improved performance, a better work-life balance and the opportunity to develop and enhance their skill-set in this contemporary way of working.

For organisations the potential benefits include; increased productivity levels, better defined personal and team performance metrics, improved individual accountability, happy and well-motivated employees, better staff retention levels, and an opportunity for a redefined work culture.

That's if we *get it right*. The ability to work from home *effectively* is key in turning this potential in to reality.

We hope you enjoyed this book and be sure to follow us at:
www.howtoworkfromhomebetter.com

Printed in Great Britain
by Amazon